CONTENTS

Part1-Wildlife Points Of Rajasthan

Part2-Lakes of Rajasthan

1. Anand Sagar Lake (Banswara)
2. Anasagar Lake (Ajmer)
3. Sardar Samand Lake And Palace (Jodhpur)
4. Jaisamand Lake (Udaipur)
5. Balsamand Lake
6. Doodh Talai Lake (Udaipur)
7. Fateh Sagar Lake (Udaipur)
8. Lake Pichola (Udaipur)
9. Badi Lake (Udaipur)
10. Gadisar Lake (Jaisalmer)
11. Amar Sagar Lake (Jaisalmer)
12. Silliserh Lake (Alwar)
13. Kodamdesar Temple And Lake (Bikaner)
14. Gajner Palace And Lake (Bikaner)
15. Darbari Lake (Bikaner)
16. Lake Jait Sagar (Bundi)
17. Lake Nawal Sagar (Bundi)
18. Lake Kanak Sagar, Dugari (Bundi)
19. Talab-E-Shahi (Dholpur)
20. Sambhar Lake (Jaipur)
21. Ranisar Padamsar (Jaisalmer)
22. Sardar Samand Lake And Palace (Jaisalmer)
23. Kailana Lake (Jaisalmer)
24. Balsamand Lake (Jaisalmer)
25. Kishorsagar Lake (Kota)

1. BAND BARETHA (BHARATPUR)

BAND BARETHA

Band Baretha is an old wildlife reserve of the rulers of Bharatpur, currently under the administration of the Forest Department. The construction of the dam on Kakund River was started by Maharaj Jaswant Singh in 1866 AD and completed by Maharaj Ram Singh in 1897 AD. The palace inside the reserve was built by Maharaj Kishan Singh and is the private property of the Bharatpur royal family. Band Baretha is a bird watcher's paradise because of over 200 species of birds, including the elusive Black Bittern.

2. KEOLADEO NATIONAL PARK
BIRD HAVEN (BHARATPUR)

Formerly known as the Bharatpur Bird Sanctuary, the Keoladeo National Park is recognised as one of the world's most important bird breeding and feeding grounds. It originated in as a royal hunting reserve during the 1850s and was a game reserve for Maharajas and the British. In fact, Lord Linlithgow, Viceroy of India from 1936 to 1943, shot over thousands of ducks with his hunting party in a single day! In 1982, Keoladeo was declared a national park and then later listed as a World Heritage Site by UNESCO in 1985. The park is home to over 370 species of birds and animals such as the basking python, painted storks, deer, nilgai and more. Noted Indian ornithologist and naturalist Salim Ali used his influence to garner government support to create Keoladeo National Park. It was also known as the breeding ground for the rare and elusive to spot Siberian crane. Keoladeo National Park offers well-defined treks which can be covered on either foot, or cycle or rickshaws. In fact, the park management has trained the rickshaw pullers in bird watching and they make for extremely knowledgeable guides.

3. DESERT NATIONAL PARK (JAISALMER)

The Desert National Park displays the best of the Thar Desert's ecosystem and its varied wildlife. The Park is formed of undulating sand dunes, jagged rocks, dense salt lake bottoms and inter-medial areas. Various species of animals such as black buck, chinkara and desert fox inhabit the Park. The highly endangered Great Indian Bustard, one of the world's heaviest flying birds, can also be seen here. In winter, the park hosts an incredible variety of migratory raptors such Himalayan and Eurasian Griffon Vultures, Eastern Imperial Eagle, and the Saker Falcon.

4. GAJNER WILDLIFE SANCTUARY (BIKANER)

Barely 32 kilometers from Bikaner, on the Jaisalmer road, is a lush green forest which is a haven to the nilgai, chinkara, black buck, wild boar, flocks of imperial sand grouse and many other species of migratory birds that make the sprawling forest their winter home.

5. KAILA DEVI SANCTUARY (KARULI)

Covered in rich and dense forests, the Kaila Devi Sanctuary begins right after the Kaila Devi Temple and extends on both the sides of the road to eventually join the Ranthambore National Park. This green reserve is home to some great natural treasures like the chinkaras, nilgai, jackals and leopards. Along with the wide variety of wildlife, one can also spot rare birds like sandpipers and kingfishers.

6. MACHIYA SAFARI PARK (JODHPUR)

This park is situated on the way to Jaisalmer, about 1 kilometer from Kailana Lake. It offers a bird watching point for visitors and is also home to several animals such as deer, desert foxes, monitor lizards, blue bulls, hare, wild cats, mongoose, monkeys, etc. The park also offers spectacular views of sunset and should not be missed.

7. MUKUNDARA TIGER RESERVE (KOTA)

The Mukundara Tiger Reserve is 50 kilometres from Kota. Tigers are often relocated here from Ranthambore Reserve. It has a core area of 417 square kilometres and a buffer zone covering 342.82 square kilometres. Other wildlife includes panther, deer, wild boar and bear. This thickly wooded area is home to a large variety of birds as well.

8. NAHARGARH BIOLOGICAL PARK (JAIPUR)

CONSERVING FLORA AND FAUNA

© Arijit Banerjee

Nahargarh Biological Park, a part of the Nahargarh sanctuary is located about 12 km from Jaipur on the Jaipur-Delhi highway. It encompasses a large area of 720 hectares and is situated under the Aravalli range. The Park is famous for its vast flora and fauna, and its main aim is to conserve it. It also doubles up as a great place to educate people and conduct research on existing flora and fauna. At Nahargarh Biological Park, ornithologists can expect to see over 285 species of birds, of which, the most popular is the white-naped tit, which can only be found here. When you visit the Park, make sure you also head to Ram Sagar, which is a famous among bird watchers and makes for a great spot to catch different varieties of birds. While here, you can stay at well-equipped and famous places such as Ganga Vilas, Gopal Vilas and Lalit Vilas, which were famous with the maharajas of the yore as hunting lodges.

The Nahargarh Zoological Park is also worth a visit and houses animals such as Asiatic lions, Bengal tigers, panthers, hyenas, wolves, deer, crocodiles, sloth bear, Himalayan black bear, wild boar, etc. The zoo is open from 15th March – 14th October between 8.30 am to 5.30 pm and from 15th October – 14th March between 9.00 am to 5.00 pm.

9. RAMGARH VISHDHARI SANCTUARY (BUNDI)

Ramgarh Vishdhari Wildlife Sanctuary is located 45 kilometres from Bundi on the Bundi-Nainwa road. Covering an area of 252 sq. km., this sanctuary is home to a variety of flora and fauna. Established in 1982, it forms a buffer for Ranthambore National Park. The best time to visit is between September and May.

10. RANTHAMBORE (SAWAI MADHOPUR)

Situated 14 km from Sawai Madhopur, the Ranthambore Park gets its name from the Ranthambore Fort situated within its boundaries. The National Park, situated amidst the Aravalis and Vindhya ranges is spreads over an area of 392 sq.km of thick forest punctuated with pleasant waterfalls. It is home to the elusive tiger, other animals found here include chinkara, sambhar, cheetal and over 300 species of birds.

11. SARISKA TIGER RESERVE (ALWAR)

Sariska Tiger Reserve is a national park where you will find a perfect intermingling of nature. It contains mountains, grasslands, dry deciduous forests and cliffs which span over 800 square kilometres. Situated in Alwar, the Tiger Reserve is nestled in the lap of Aravali hills. Currently home to numerous animals apart from tigers, the reserve showcases nature in its best form. Animals like jungle cats, rhesus macaque, sambhar, chital, wild boar, etc., are found here. Not only animals, you get to see a number of bird species, such as sand grouse, harbor quails, crested serpent eagles, etc. here as well.

When you go on a jeep safari at Sariska tiger reserve, you can spot beautiful animals going about their day, especially tigers. Not only this, you can visit the Kankwadi fort, a place that could also be visited only by jeep safari. You also get to go bird watching while on the safari as the reserve is home to more than 220 species of birds with migratory birds from Europe, Central Asia, and other regions. Going on a safari can prove to be highly enjoyable if you go in groups as it would add an entirely different level of fun quotient to the trip.

NEELKANTH TEMPLE

On an isolated mountain in Sariska Tiger Reserve stands the Neelkanth temple. Built in the 6 th century, the temple has a collection of erotic statues. Bearing a similarity to Khajuraho, the temple is a famous tourist attraction.

PANDUPOL HANUMAN TEMPLE

Another temple located inside the temple premises is the Pandupol Hanuman Temple. The temple stands amidst a scenic waterfall. Having a mythological link with Mahabharata, the temple is visited by people to relax by the waterfall and also perform pilgrimage activities. Sariska Tiger Reserve is a destination with many architectural and natural spots that one can explore. The place is a magnet for travel enthusiasts, especially wildlife lovers. Romanticize with nature and spot mighty tigers for an exhilarating experience at the tiger reserve.

12. SHERGARH SANCTUARY (BARAN)

The perfect destination for nature lovers, Shergarh sanctuary is located in Shergarh village, about 65 km from Baran district. Rich in flora and fauna, Shergarh sanctuary is home to several endangered species of plants, as well as tigers, sloth bears, leopards and wild boards, among other animals. A photographer's delight, Shergarh sanctuary is easily accessible by road.

13. SORSAN WILDLIFE SANCTUARY

Located 50 km from Kota is the Sorsan Wildlife Sanctuary. Popularly known as the Sorsan Grasslands, it is a 41 sq.km bird sanctuary which is home to scrubby vegetation, numerous water bodies and a vast variety of birds and animals. Visitors here can hope to catch a glimpse of orioles, quails, partridges, robins, weavers, greylag geese, common pochards, teals and pintails. Come winter and flocks of migrant birds such as warblers, flycatchers, larks, starlings and rosy pastors fly here. You can also spot animals such as black buck and gazelles.

14. TAL CHHAPAR SANCTUARY (CHURU)

Renowned for being a safe haven black bucks and a variety of birds, this sanctuary is named after the Chhapar village. Located in the Sujangarh Tehsil of Churu, it is 210 km from Jaipur. Its open grasslands scattered with trees give it the appearance of a savannah. The sanctuary is a bird watcher's paradise as it is home to birds such as eastern imperial eagle, black ibis, demoiselle cranes, skylarks, ring doves and more. One can also spot the desert fox and desert cat here.

15. VAN VIHAR SANCTUARY (DHOLPUR)

One of the oldest wildlife reserves of the rulers of Dholpur, Van Vihar Sanctuary is spread over an area of about 25 sq. km over the Vindhyan Plateau. The sanctuary is characterised by a wide range of fascinating flora and fauna that grabs the tourists' attention. Endowed with animals like sambhar, chital, blue bull, wild boar, sloth bear, hyena and leopard, the Van Vihar Sanctuary is very popular among nature lovers visiting Dholpur.

16. SAJJANGARH BIOLOGICAL PARK (UDAIPUR)

Located just outside the Sajjangarh Wildlife Sanctuary, at the foot hills of Bans-Dahara hills is the Sajjangarh Biological Park spread over 36 hectares of land. In this park one can see the Carnivores and Herbivores animals moving around in their natural habitat. One can visit the Park on foot or by Golf car on payment basis.

LAKES
OF
RAJASTHAN

1. ANAND SAGAR LAKE (BANSWARA)

This artificial lake, also known as Bai Talab was constructed by Lanchi Bai, the Rani of Maharaval Jagmal Singh. Located in the eastern part of Banswara, it is surrounded by holy trees known as 'Kalpa Vriksha', famous for fulfilling the wishes of visitors. The 'chattris' or cenotaphs of the rulers of the state are also scattered nearby.

2. ANASAGAR LAKE (AJMER)

Anasagar Lake is a scenic artificial lake, commissioned and built by Arnoraj Chauhan, son of Ajaypal Chauhan, between 1135 and 1150 AD. Arnoraj was also known as Anaji, which gives the lake its name. Many years later, Mughal Emperor Jahangir added his touch to the lake by laying out the Daulat Bagh Gardens near the lake. Emperor Shah Jahan too, contributed to the expansion by building five pavilions, known as the Baradari, between the garden and the lake.

3. SARDAR SAMAND LAKE AND PALACE (JODHPUR)

Built on the banks of the Sardar Samand Lake by Maharaja Umaid Singh in 1933, the Sardar Samand Lake Palace is a spectacular hunting lodge. It remains the royal family's favourite retreat and houses a vast collection of African trophies and original watercolour paintings. The lake attracts several migratory and local birds such as the yellow-legged green pigeon, Himalayan griffon and Dalmatian pelican, making it a bird watcher's paradise.

4. JAISAMAND LAKE (UDAIPUR)

THE SECOND LARGEST ARTIFICIAL LAKE IN INDIA

Jaisamand Lake is renowned for being the second largest artificial lake in Asia. In fact, it used to be the largest artificial lake in Asia until Aswan Dam in Egypt was not constructed. Located at a distance of 48 kilometres from the city of Udaipur, it is also known as Dhebar. In 1685, Maharana Jai Singh built this lake during the construction of a dam on the Gomti River. Jaisamand Lake covers an area of 36 square kilometres, it stretches to a length of 14 kilometres and width of 9 kilometres. The massive dam was constructed on this lake also houses a centrally located Shiva temple. The summer palace of the queen of Udaipur forms a perfect backdrop to the Lake. There are six, intricately carved marble cenotaphs on its embankment. Jaisamand Lake comprises seven islands, of which, one is still inhabited by the tribe of Bhil Minas. Graceful marble steps lead to the water and you can enjoy a lovely boat ride in the mesmerizing waters. Jaisamand Lake is close to the Jaisamand Sanctuary which serves as habitat to various types of birds, panthers, leopards, deer, wild boars and crocodiles. It is definitely worth a visit.

5. BALSAMAND LAKE

Balsamand Lake is about 5 kilometres from Jodhpur on the Jodhpur-Mandore Road. Built in 1159 AD, it was planned as a water reservoir to cater to Mandore. The Balsamand Lake Palace was built on its shore later as a summer palace. It is surrounded by lush green gardens that house groves of trees such as mango, papaya, pomegranate, guava and plum. Animals and birds like the jackal and peacock also call this place home. This lake is now a popular picnic spot with tourists and locals.

6. DOODH TALAI LAKE (UDAIPUR)

The road that takes visitors to Pichola Lake has another popular destination – the Doodh Talai Lake. The lake is nestled between several small hillocks which themselves are tourist attractions. The Deen Dayal Upadhyay Park and the Manikya Lal Verma Garden are part of the Doodh Talai Lake Garden.

7. FATEH SAGAR LAKE (UDAIPUR)

This delightful lake, bordered by hills and woodlands, lies to the north of Lake Pichola. This artificial lake is connected to Lake Pichola by a canal. The lake houses the beautiful Nehru Island as well as an islet on which stands the Udaipur Solar Observatory. It was inaugurated by the Duke of Connaught and was initially called Connaught Bundh.

8. LAKE PICHOLA (UDAIPUR)

Picholi was the name of a village that lent its name to the lake. The islands of Jagniwas and Jagmandir are housed in this lake. Along the eastern banks of the lake lies the City Palace. A boat ride in the lake around sunset offers a breathtaking view of the Lake and City Palace.

9. BADI LAKE (UDAIPUR)

Badi Lake is an artificial lake that was built by Maharana Raj Singh to help the city counterbalance the devastating effects of drought. He named the lake Jiyan Sagar after his mother Jana Devi. During the drought of 1973, the lake proved to be a blessing for the people of Udaipur. And today, the lake has become a popular attraction in the city, for both locals and tourists. Surrounded by three chhatris, the Badi Lake is one of the finest fresh water lakes in the country, and is counted among the major tourist attractions in Udaipur. Located about 12 km from the city, the ambiance of the lake is calm and tranquil, and offers a scenic respite from the hustle and bustle of city life.

10. GADISAR LAKE (JAISALMER)

Laser Water Show at Gadisar Lake is one of the first and largest Laser Water Show having water screen projection mapping using 3-chip DLP projectors of 25,000 lumens. Show depicts story of founders of Jaisalmer city, Jaisalmer fort, attacks of invaders on the fort & sacrifice of brave Rajput to save their land, glimpses of other tourist locations in Jaisalmer region e.g. Tanot Mata Temple, Lodruva Temple, Laxminarayan Temple, Longowala war scenes, etc.

11. AMAR SAGAR LAKE (JAISALMER)

Amar Sagar Lake, located about 7 km towards the western outskirts of Jaisalmer, is a lake cum oasis lying adjacent to the Amar Singh Palace. The palace itself was built in the 17 th century. The complex that includes the palace and the lake is also home to several ponds and wells, along with an old temple dedicated to Lord Shiva. Numerous figureheads of animals carved in stone surround the lake, and according to legends, these carved figureheads are supposed to be protectors of the royal family. At one end, there are pavilions with stairs that lead down to the lake; while at the other end is a beautiful, aesthetically carved Jain temple. A peaceful and tranquil place, the Amar Sagar Lake is yet another spot in Jaisalmer where you have an opportunity to watch a gorgeous sunset.

12. SILLISERH LAKE (ALWAR)

Located 15 kilometres to the southwest of Alwar, this tranquil lake is nestled amidst forested hills and boasts of magnificent cenotaphs on its bank. In 1845, Maharaja Vinay Singh constructed a hunting chalet here for his Queen, Shila. Today it is a tourist bungalow.

13. KODAMDESAR TEMPLE AND LAKE (BIKANER)

24 kilometres from Bikaner is the Kodamdesar Temple. Kodamdesar Bhainru Ji was installed by Rao Bikaji sometime during the first three years of his arrival from Jodhpur. This place of worship was initially chosen as the site to lay the foundation of Bikaner, but was later shifted to its present location. A Beautiful lake is situated in the backyard of this temple. The serenity and tranquility of this lake memorize the devotees and the Tourists.

14. GAJNER PALACE AND LAKE (BIKANER)

© VINAY JOSHI

Gajner is an incomparable jewel of the Thar. The Gajner Palace was founded by Maharaja Gaj Singh ji of Bikaner in the year 1784, and then completed by the great Maharaja Ganga Singh of Bikaner on the banks of the lake. It was meant to serve as a hunting and relaxing lodge for the royal family as well as for visiting guests. It has now been converted into a hotel

15. DARBARI LAKE (BIKANER)

This lake is situated on Bikaner Jaisalmer Highway 33 KM far away from Bikaner city. This lake has the reputation of most popular picnic spot during the monsoon among the local people as well as tracking lover. Beauty of the lush green catchment area and ample water is something one most experience.

16. LAKE JAIT SAGAR (BUNDI)

Located close to the Taragarh Fort, this picturesque lake is surrounded by hills and covered with pretty lotus flowers that bloom during winter and monsoon.

17.   LAKE NAWAL SAGAR (BUNDI)

Nawal Sagar Lake is an artificial lake that is a major tourist attraction and can even be seen from the Taragarh Fort. There is a half-submerged temple dedicated to Lord Varun Dev in its centre. What makes the lake unique is that one can see the reflection of nearby palaces and forts in its waters.

18. LAKE KANAK SAGAR, DUGARI (BUNDI)

About 48 kilometres from the town of Bundi lies this wonderful flat lake. There is also a town named after the lake. One can spot several migratory birds here such as bar headed goose and Demoille cranes all through the year.

19. TALAB-E-SHAHI (DHOLPUR)

Talab-e-Shahi as the name suggests is a picturesque lake situated 27 km from Dholpur, and 5 km from Bari in Rajasthan. Both the lake and the palace were originally built as a shooting lodge for Prince Shah Jahan in the year 1617 A.D. The beauty and the location of this beautiful lake invites a number of winter migratory fowl such as pintail, red crested pochard, common pochard, tufted duck and pigeon.

20.   SAMBHAR LAKE (JAIPUR)

Sambhar Lake is one of the largest inland salt lake and lies just 70 kms from Jaipur. It is an incredible landscape, almost resembling the Rann of Kutch, Gujarat. Apart from producing a large percentage of India's salt supply - it also an incredible place to spot birds including large flocks of flamingos. The views from the Shakambhari Mata Temple are breathtaking at sunset and one can spend hours in solitude. Another unique aspect is the Saltwork's own railway system built to transfer salt from the pans to the processing unit. A visit to the salt lake and a walk in the Sambhar town is also a must do activity. Devyani Kund, Sharmishtha Sarovar, Salt Museum, Circuit House, etc are also important places to visit in Sambhar. One can also visit religious sites Naraina & Bhairana on the way to Sambhar.

21. RANISAR PADAMSAR (JAISALMER)

Located near the Fateh Pole in Mehrangarh, the Ranisar and Padmasar are adjacent lakes that were constructed in the year 1459. Ranisar Lake was built on orders of Queen Jasmade Hadi, Rao Jodha's wife while Padmasar Lake was ordered by Queen Padmini of Rao Ganga, daughter of Rana Sanga of Mewar.

22. SARDAR SAMAND LAKE AND PALACE (JAISALMER)

Built on the banks of the Sardar Samand Lake by Maharaja Umaid Singh in 1933, the Sardar Samand Lake Palace is a spectacular hunting lodge. It remains the royal family's favourite retreat and houses a vast collection of African trophies and original watercolour paintings. The lake attracts several migratory and local birds such as the yellow-legged green pigeon, Himalayan griffon and Dalmatian pelican, making it a bird watcher's paradise.

23. KAILANA LAKE (JAISALMER)

Situated on Jaisalmer road, this small artificial lake is an ideal picnic spot. It is like a canvas with a splash of romantic colours. The beauty of the lake stays with you long after you've experienced it. For those who'd like to go out on to the lake, boating facilities are also available through R.T.D.C.

24. BALSAMAND LAKE (JAISALMER)

Balsamand Lake is about 5 kilometres from Jodhpur on the Jodhpur-Mandore Road. Built in 1159 AD, it was planned as a water reservoir to cater to Mandore. The Balsamand Lake Palace was built on its shore later as a summer palace. It is surrounded by lush green gardens that house groves of trees such as mango, papaya, pomegranate, guava and plum. Animals and birds like the jackal and peacock also call this place home. This lake is now a popular picnic spot with tourists and locals.

25.   KISHORSAGAR LAKE (KOTA)

Kisorsagar Lake is one of the many lakes and ponds commissioned by the rulers of Kota. Jagmandir was built in later half of 18th century as retreat for the royal family of kota. Presently a boat service is available for the visitors to go to Jagmandir and enjoy a magnificent view of surrounding Kota city from there.

26.   PUSHKAR LAKE (AJMER)

According to Hindu scriptures, the sacred Pushkar Lake is described as 'Tirtha Raj', the king of all pilgrimage sites. No pilgrimage is considered to be complete without a dip in in the holy Pushkar Lake. Semi-circular in shape and about 8-10 metres deep, Pushkar Lake is surrounded by 52 bathing ghats and over 400 temples and is truly a magnificent sight to behold.

Printed in Great Britain
by Amazon

29386051R00026